RACHEL
Turns Her Passion Into a Business

Words by Erica Swallow
Pictures by Li Zeng

Entrepreneur
Kid

For Maria, Alice, and Nick, friends who keep me grounded and inspired.
— E.S.

To my parents and Casper for believing in me.
— L.Z.

Text copyright © 2017 Erica Swallow ● Illustrations copyright © 2017 Li Zeng ● All rights reserved. Published in 2017 by Entrepreneur Kid in Little Rock, Arkansas 72201. ● No portion of this book may be reproduced, stored in a retrieval system, or transmitted in any form or by any means, mechanical, electronic, photocopying, recording, or otherwise, without written permission from the publisher. For permissions, write to hi@entrepreneurkid.com. ● Printed in China.● Library of Congress Cataloging-in-Publication Data ● Names: Swallow, Erica, author. | Zeng, Li, 1988-, illustrator. ● Title: Rachel turns her passion into a business / by Erica Swallow ; illustrated by Li Zeng.● Series: Entrepreneur Kid. ● Description: Redwood City, CA: Entrepreneur Kid, 2017. ● Identifiers: ISBN 978-1-946984-03-6 (Hardcover) | 978-1-946984-06-7 (pbk.) | 978-1-946984-07-4 (ebook) | LCCN 2017939662 ● Summary: Teen lacrosse player Rachel Zietz takes an entrepreneurship course and realizes she can blend business and fun by creating a lacrosse equipment company. ● Subjects: LCSH Zietz, Rachel. | Young businesspeople--Juvenile literature. | Businesspeople--United States--Biography--Juvenile literature. | Entrepreneurship--Juvenile literature. | Small business--Juvenile literature. | Lacrosse--Juvenile literature. ● BISAC JUVENILE NONFICTION / General | JUVENILE NONFICTION / Business & Economics | JUVENILE NONFICTION / Careers | JUVENILE NONFICTION / Sports & Recreation / General ● Classification: LCC HC102.5. Z56 2017 | DDC 338.04/092--dc23 ● Printed in China ● First printing, June 2017 ● The text type was set in Capriola and NTR. ● The display text was set in Bungee Outline and Ranchers. ● The illustrations were created using Adobe Illustrator. ● Special thank you to design interns Logan Melton, Shiori Soya, and Zhifang Wang for assistance with art.

Rachel Zietz is one of the most fierce athletes at her school. She plays lacrosse and can cover almost any position on the field.

She plays on three lacrosse teams and practices every day after school. There's nothing she loves more than tossing around the ball with her teammates.

It took her a while to discover her passion for the game. She tried almost every other sport before trying lacrosse: Basketball, tennis, soccer, and even flag football!

Young
Entrepreneurs
Academy

If there's one word to describe Rachel, it's competitive. Her teammates know that she's up for any challenge.

Since she was four years old, Rachel would go with her father to work to see what running a business is like.

She would bring her briefcase and organize his office while he had important meetings and phone calls.

Running a business always seemed like a grown-up thing to do. Rachel had never seen any kids starting companies.

When she visited her father's office, she was always the only kid there.

On TV, there were no kid business owners. And none of her friends were business owners, either.

Rachel started to believe that being a business owner was only something adults could do.

Young
Entrepreneurs
Academy

Learn to be an entrepreneur this year!

One day, Rachel learned about a class that could teach her how to be an entrepreneur, someone who starts a business. It was for kids, and she was just old enough to participate!

Maybe I am too young?

Rachel wasn't sure what kind of business she could start. "Maybe I'm too young," she told herself.

If Rachel was going to participate, she wanted to come prepared with an idea.

Every day after school while practicing at home, she thought about what business she could build. But no ideas came to her.

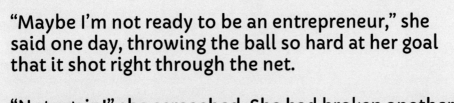

"Maybe I'm not ready to be an entrepreneur," she said one day, throwing the ball so hard at her goal that it shot right through the net.

"Not again!" she screeched. She had broken another goal with her powerful shot.

At dinner that night, Rachel was nervous. Her entrepreneurship classes started the next day, and she still didn't have an idea. Plus, she had broken yet another lacrosse goal. She wanted to make her family proud.

Dinner went unexpectedly well. Rachel's mom said class would be fine tomorrow, and her dad said the goal wasn't that great from the start. Her brother and sister were too busy enjoying dessert to even notice Rachel was upset.

The next day, business classes were packed. Rachel sat in class, and the first speaker took the stage. "The biggest question you need to answer is: What problem do you want to solve?" she said.

Suddenly, Rachel's idea came to her: "I want to make better goals and practice equipment for lacrosse! Goals so strong they don't break!"

During that first week, she thought of a hundred other ideas, but no idea topped her lacrosse business idea!

Weeks went by, and Rachel learned the ins and outs of business.

She designed her products...

Looked for a factory to make them...

Chose a good price for her goods...

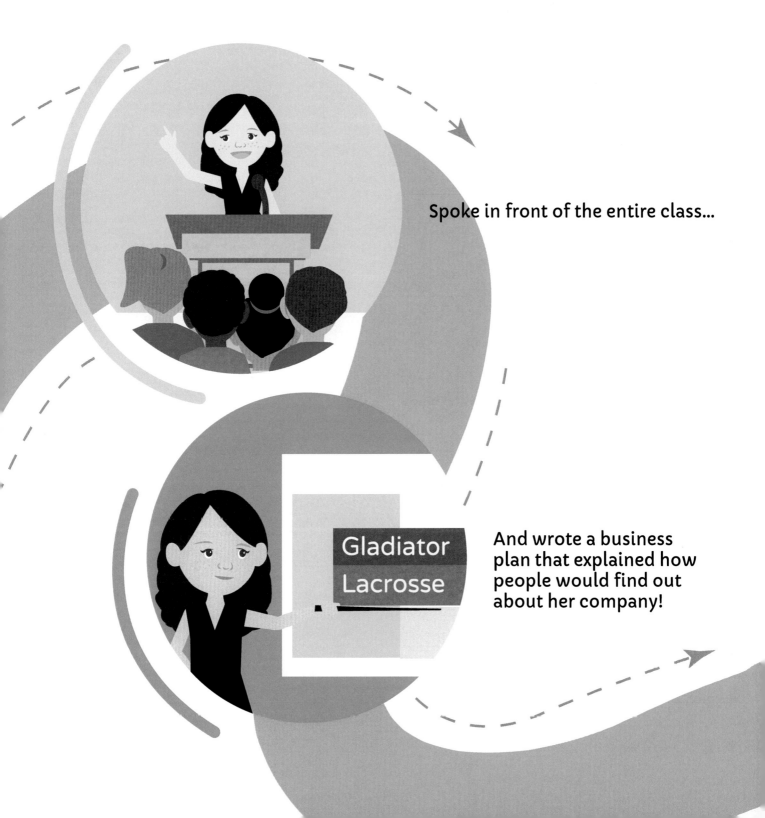

Spoke in front of the entire class...

Gladiator Lacrosse

And wrote a business plan that explained how people would find out about her company!

Rachel was nervous, but during her first class competition, she finally realized that starting a business was for her. Everyone pitched their business ideas to grown-up business owners. When the top winner was chosen...

It was Rachel!

Rachel Zietz

1st Place

On the final day of class, too, she gained a lot of the confidence she had been missing. Everyone pitched for the chance to win funds to help them start their businesses. The top winner was announced...

It was Rachel!

Rachel Zietz

It turns out, Rachel knew a lot about business! She felt proud of her accomplishments.

"I can do this!" she exclaimed.

Her parents and mentors had believed in her, but she hadn't done the same. It even started to feel like the whole world believed in her!

ANK

30 Most
Influential Teens
of 2016

Rachel Zietz

Lacrosse Star
Casey Powell Teams
Up with Rachel Zietz

SOUTH FLORIDA
BUSINESS JOURNAL

How 14-year-old Rachel Zietz
built a $1 million company

Rachel started her business and placed the first product order. Her lacrosse equipment was so popular that she had to hire more people to help run the business!

Today, Rachel even works with her favorite professional lacrosse player, Casey Powell, who she watched on TV when she was younger.

They designed a special line of equipment that's now available in huge stores across the country.

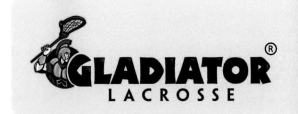

Since those days back in her father's office, Rachel knew she wanted to start a business when she got older, but she didn't know she could start one while she was a kid.

Rachel now tells kids everywhere that anything is possible if you believe in yourself.

Now it's your turn...
What problems do you want to solve in the world?

Author's Note by Erica Swallow

"Rachel Turns Her Passion Into a Business" is a story about the entrepreneurial journey of Rachel Zietz, real-life founder and CEO of Gladiator Lacrosse®, a lacrosse equipment company.

The book documents Rachel's story and how the worlds of sports and business collide when she enrolls in the Young Entrepreneurs Academy (YEA!) program at the Boca Raton Chamber of Commerce. Co-sponsored by the chamber and Florida Atlantic University, YEA! opens her eyes to her potential to become a business owner.

Rachel's desire to found Gladiator Lacrosse stems from her clear passion for the sport of lacrosse. She started playing in fifth grade, when after trying basketball, tennis, soccer, and flag football, she realized lacrosse was the sport for her. Eventually, her love of lacrosse and issues she faced with practice equipment led to her founding Gladiator Lacrosse in 2012 when she was 13 years old.

A native of Boca Raton, Florida, Rachel grew up in an entrepreneurial family and around business. Her father, Sam Zietz, is the CEO of point of sale systems vendor TouchSuite, while her mother, Sheila Zietz is a corporate attorney. Even her younger brother, Jordan, is an entrepreneur, as founder and CEO of GameReef, a video game console rental company. He founded the company at 13 years old after going through the 33-week Boca Raton YEA! program Rachel completed. Little sister Morgan hasn't yet caught the entrepreneurial bug, but she enjoys art and has followed in Rachel's footsteps, becoming a lacrosse player in the second grade, as a goalie. With a love for design, Morgan occasionally helps Rachel on Gladiator Lacrosse designs, particularly within apparel offerings.

Rachel Zietz plays lacrosse. Photo: Harry Jordan

All of Rachel's business exposure aside, she never thought she would be a teen entrepreneur. Even after enrolling in YEA!, where she was the youngest participant in her cohort, she didn't expect to found a business. She was in seventh grade, 12 years old, and intimidated by all of the high schoolers around her. In interviews, she told me that she was just planning to finish the program and move on.

She hit a tipping point, though, when she won the program's elevator pitch competition. She told me during our first interview she realized at that point, "Just because I'm this young, doesn't mean I can't stack up against these older kids and be successful!" She hit the ground running from there, writing the business plan and collaborating with professional sports designers on product designs. By the end of the program, she had everything in place — she ordered a 45-foot container of Gladiator Lacrosse's first offerings: Goals and rebounders.

Today, Gladiator Lacrosse is a multi-million dollar business, having generated $200,000 in revenue in its first year of operation. As of 2016, it was on track to clear $2 million for the year. Gladiator Lacrosse products are distributed online and in large chain retailer DICK'S Sporting Goods stores across America.

The company offers better-quality products — thicker netting and metals for longer-lasting practice gear — at affordable prices. It also collaborated with Rachel's favorite lacrosse player, Casey Powell, to develop a "Casey Powell Signature Edition" of equipment that comes in a sleek black design with a stylized Casey Powell signature and emblem. Rachel describes Casey as her "number one idol as a kid," proving that anything is possible when you dream big. The company also makes apparel and has aspirations to release more products, including headgear that prevents player concussions.

Rachel was recognized as TIME's Most Influential Teens of 2016, sandwiched between Olympic gymnast Laurie Hernandez and Sasha and Malia Obama, daughters of U.S. President Barack Obama. Rachel has appeared on ABC's *Shark Tank*; was a finalist for Greater Miami Chamber of Commerce's 2015 Entrepreneur Award; and has received coverage in *The New York Times* and *The Wall Street Journal*, among other outlets.

While writing this book, illustrator Li Zeng, videographer Dan Ndombe, and I visited Rachel, her family, and the Boca Raton Chamber of Commerce. The story and pictures you've encountered in this book were all inspired by in-person and online interviews with key influencers and supporters. To learn more about Rachel and her company, visit entrepreneurkid.com and gladiatorlacrosse.com. Both sites feature videos, photos, and more information about the making of Gladiator Lacrosse equipment and the Entrepreneur Kid book about Rachel's entrepreneurial journey. For information on Young Entrepreneurs Academy programs near you, visit yeausa.org.

Rachel Zietz with Gladiator Lacrosse rebounder and goal. Photo: Gladiator Lacrosse

The Zietz family. Photo: Dan Ndombe

How many Entrepreneur Kid books have you read?

There are four books in the Entrepreneur Kid series. Read them all to learn how other kids like you started their own businesses. You, too, can be an Entrepreneur Kid by solving problems around you.

Go to entrepreneurkid.com to buy the full series and submit your Entrepreneur Kid story for an opportunity to be featured on our website!

Find Entrepreneur Kid on social media to share your reading experience.

@EntrepreneurKid   @EntrepreneurKid   /EntrepreneurKid   /company/EntrepreneurKid

Made in the USA
Lexington, KY
27 September 2017